BIBLICAL
SONSHIP

AN EVALUATION OF THE
SONSHIP™ DISCIPLESHIP COURSE

JAY E. ADAMS

TIMELESS TEXTS
Woodruff, SC

Contents

Preface

Does your Christian life satisfy? Are you looking for something more? Something that will transcend the struggles that you now endure day by day?

If so, you are a likely candidate for Sonship™. This teaching that appeals to Christians who are failing to live as they ought maintains that most of the church has been sadly in error by viewing the gospel merely as the way in which one is saved from the penalty of sin; instead, it ought to be viewed also as the fundamental dynamic for living the Christian life.

Moreover, it holds that most Christians find themselves living as orphans, although God, in union with Christ, has made them Sons. It claims that a person can change this sad state of affairs by continuing to preach the gospel to himself and by repenting and believing over and over again. It teaches that not only justification, but also sanctification, is by faith in the good news.

Certainly if it is true that God has raised up Sonship™ to "return" the church to such teaching, we all ought to join up on the spot. But the question is whether or not Sonship is truly a help. That is to say, is it biblical? Or is it just another aberration in the church? Is it more likely to help or hinder the work of Jesus Christ? To answer these questions is the sole purpose of this book.

Chapter One

Why This Book?

Unlike many others, this is a book that I had no interest in writing. But everywhere I go, it seems, someone is asking me about "Sonship." Most of these inquiries (they have come by way of letter, phone, and word of mouth) express some sense of uneasiness about the movement, but the questioner seems to have a hard time putting his finger on just what it is, if anything, that is wrong. I hear such statements as "I'm hearing the same thing from the pulpit every week," "It gets boring after a while," and "What is this Sonship teaching anyway? It seems so vague." One woman who listened to Sonship tapes wrote, "I made notes as I listened to the tapes. Both Jack and his wife seemed to ramble. . . . If my notes seem to be confusing and disjointed that is because that is the way the tapes were given." A pastor in Pennsylvania sent me some information about Sonship, saying that it was confusing and that he was very hesitant to go along with it. People have urged me to write about the movement. Sonship teaching has invaded my own denomination. I am concerned about its uncritical adoption in Christian circles. All of these considerations, and more, have *pushed* me into publishing.

There are various problems connected with Sonship that I will point out in this book. None of them are peripheral. Because they relate so clearly to the central fact of the Christian faith—the gospel of Jesus Christ—we cannot avoid discussing them. There are many other unfortunate teachings not so central, but important, that also pertain to this movement which is gaining ground (especially) in Reformed denominations. There is no question in my mind that the proponents of Sonship are well meaning and wish only to help. They are captivated by their

1

beliefs and want to influence the entire church if they can. They
envision their mission as awakening the church to neglected
truth to which, as they put it, we must "return." In a promotional
pamphlet advertising a Sonship "Phone Discipleship Course,"
the following claim is made:

> The issues of our personal and corporate Sonship are
> central to the advance of the gospel. It has a pro-
> found impact on how we worship, plant churches,
> evangelize and disciple believers. It affects how we
> live with and love our families, our friends and our
> neighbor[s].

Plainly, advocates of Sonship see their mission and teaching as
global in scope, indeed as the most vital element in Christian life
and ministry. Yet according to them, the message they teach has
been virtually lost to the church. They see themselves in the
position of restoring it. There is more than a bit of an exclusiv-
ism to these claims that is not only dangerous but also almost
cultic. The excessive zeal with which this teaching is promoted,
the goals of changing how people worship, conduct their marriages, preach, and grow in their faith all demand our close
examination and biblical evaluation.

Moreover, the pamphlet goes on to say that Sonshippers
claim there is nothing unique about their teaching theologically;
but they say that "Sonship changes us as it makes *real* contact
with our *real* lives."[1] Sonship ought to be able to back up this
bold claim *scripturally*—not by mere anecdotal testimony or the
stories of its founders. We must call upon them to demonstrate
biblically that their claim to apply common theological teaching
in more vital ways than others holds up; in addition, we must ask
them why it is that until the Millers introduced Sonship™, others
who supposedly held to the same theology did not live in a man-

---

[1] In a pamphlet advertising the "Sonship Phone Discipling Course."

ner that was "real." Indeed, they must do more: they must clearly identify what this "real" Christian living and ministry is over against ersatz Christian living and ministry. And they must prove exegetically that the real Christian living they advocate is something the Bible itself teaches. If the claim holds up, it is stupendous; we all had better get on board. If it is false, it is likely to lead its disciples into greater despair than they had before adopting it; then we all had better *continue* to avoid it!

According to Sonship, the gospel has been neglected by the church. That is a very serious charge—one not to be leveled lightly. In teaching people that faith in the good news that Christ died for our sins and rose from the dead saves, preachers and others, according to Sonshippers, have neglected to *add* that one must "continue to preach the gospel to himself"[1] throughout life and that he must "understand and apply the gospel as the ongoing power for living the Christian life" (as another pamphlet published by World Harvest Mission[2] maintains). In short, we must see if all the hype holds up scripturally. I shall make an attempt to do just that in this book. But first, a word about the background of Sonship.

---

[1] A statement that in one form or another occurs throughout the *Sonship*™ *Manual*.

[2] The mission founded by Jack Miller.

Chapter Two

What's Behind Sonship?

This chapter is out of character for me. Ordinarily, I focus on beliefs, theories, systems and the like; not on persons. While I have considered it important to mention the names of persons associated with certain beliefs so as to help the reader identify those who teach them, my emphasis has always been on the teaching, not on the teacher. Past readers of my writings will attest to this.

In the present case, however, things are different, and for good reasons. Although I find it irksome to do so, at the outset I am forced to discuss something of the experiences of Jack and Rose Marie Miller themselves. "Why do it if it is so distasteful to you?" I want to answer that question right away, since it is in the background of every word I write in this chapter.

I have not attempted a personal analysis of the Millers because of animosity or bad feelings toward them, or anything of the sort. Nothing could be farther from the truth. Indeed, if anything, I have always admired Jack in many ways. The sole reason for departing from my usual custom in writing is that in describing Sonship the Millers *themselves* have so tied its origins and their teachings to their personal experiences, that it is not possible to fully understand their beliefs apart from them. The Millers have so wrapped themselves up in Sonship that the teaching is explained by their struggles and the attempted resolutions of those struggles as they experienced both.

First, let me say that I knew Jack and Rose Marie personally, have been entertained in their home at meals, and taught with Jack as a professor in the same department at Westminster Theological Seminary in Philadelphia. Jack and I never had any falling out with one another, and he and I maintained a cordial relationship (though in later years we saw little of one another) until his death.

Jack was always out of step with the other members of the Westminster faculty. Though he may have tried to be, he was not a team player. His strong emphasis on evangelism, which was one of his most attractive qualities so far as I am concerned, often led him in different directions from others who were more academically inclined. This divergence was always apparent in conversations with him, in his interests and activities, as well as in his teaching. This is a vivid recollection that grows out of many conversations with Jack and out of reports by a number of his students. He often had little time for the sorts of concerns that were the prime interests of others members of the Westminster faculty. Being something of a maverick myself, and not always sympathetic to pedantic, academic ways, I often found myself aligning with Jack. I remember, at his request, holding a discussion with some members of his church who were being hassled by people from a heretical cult. Together with some forty seminary students, we both eagerly participated in a course I designed that had as its purpose the founding of a church in Doylestown. So you can see, in some senses we were birds of a feather.

Yet, there was always something about Jack that made me hesitate to get too close to him. At the time I could not put my finger on it. But for some reason I found myself holding back. Now, since reading Sonship materials, in which Jack and Rose Marie detail some of their experiences during that period of time, I can better understand why I developed this reticence. It is these very things that pushed me away that also led them into their Sonship ideas. At the time when we worked together at Westminster Theological Seminary, Sonship did not exist, as the Sonship *Manual* makes clear. But the same factors that ultimately evolved into the movement were already percolating.

What were these factors? How did they lead the Millers to develop their doctrines? Let me mention at least some of the impressions that memory and the study of Sonship have left with me.

First, Jack always impressed me as a greatly dissatisfied person. All of us had our dissatisfactions, of course. That is to be expected in an imperfect world viewed by imperfect persons. But, in Jack, this dissatisfaction not only seemed exaggerated but also was the power that drove him in just about everything he did.[1] He seemed to consider himself a man on a mission—that much always was clear—but the mission seemed ill-defined. Jack was searching for a way in which to crystallize it.

Second, mixed together with that search, though again not sharply articulated, there was a desire for *something more*. Jack never seemed satisfied with getting more of the something he had, as perhaps the rest of us were. So, when he started a church along with his teaching, when he founded a mission, or when he eventually developed his Sonship thrust, these things were no surprise. Given the intensity of his search, some such eventualities were certain.

Third, it was my growing impression, confirmed by Sonship doctrine, that Jack had a pietistic strain in him. I mean that there was an experiential emphasis that—I regret to say—protruded (I almost said "paraded") itself before others. There was always—as there is in talks in the Sonship manual—a somewhat embarrassing confessional quality to a conversation with Jack. That is to say, if you talked very long with him, he would soon be discussing matters that pertained to himself and to his family. He seemed to see everything through his own experience. I can remember feeling uneasy during such conversations. This uneasiness did not stem from the fact that I disliked listening to facts

---

[1] Jack put it this way, "I didn't like my denomination, I didn't like my seminary, and I didn't like the church I served." Obviously, he was a dissatisfied person (*Manual*, 11-8.).

about other people's lives (I have spent countless hours doing
that very thing in counseling), but from the strong impression
that if I didn't do the same, Jack would look on me as an inau-
thentic person. Now, perhaps, I can see why that judgment may
not have been entirely correct; he may have been seeking help in
finding his way. It may have been difficult for him to simply ask.
At any rate, he never did ask for any such help.[1] So, rightly or
wrongly, because I believed that he wanted to talk rather than to
ask or listen, I never offered help.

Fourth, Jack was not easily approached. He was likable
enough, but was not the sort of person with whom one (or at
least I) could become "chummy." Indeed, Jack and Rose Marie's
lives were always so tightly bound up together that there was
rarely time for others to get close if they had wanted to. At the
time, I had no idea that this was because they were attempting to
resolve the terrible tensions they related in the Sonship *Manual*.
Now, having read about this struggle in which they were
engaged at the time, I can better understand what was happening
and why I entertained a certain apprehension about trying to
grow closer to them.

That Jack and Rose Marie (at least Jack) as much as possible
attempted to conduct a joint ministry may not have been so
much because they were trying to solve the personal problems
that they recalled in the *Manual* together, but perhaps, rather, it
was that the very closeness itself led to many of these struggles.
Perhaps Jack should have considered his call his and Rose
Marie's call hers.[2]

In her talks, reproduced in the *Manual*, Rose Marie speaks
repeatedly about how she resisted Jack's attempts to draw her

---

[1] Jack was a very unhappy person. He said "I felt that I was a failure as a
teacher, pastor, and a Christian." He went on to say that at one point he "cried
for two weeks" (*Manual*, 11-8).

[2] This was an unhappy ministry for many reasons. Jack and his wife didn't
agree on what Jack was doing. Evidently he went ahead and did it anyway,

into ministries in which she did not wish to participate. Jack, it seems, made too little a distinction between his call and ordination to the ministry and his wife's call to be his wife. At one time she recalls how he deeply embarrassed her by publicly announcing (on the spot over a Public Address system, without any warning) that she would address a group in Uganda about "how a Christian Marriage really works."[1] And this, it seems, was during the very time when they themselves were going through very difficult struggles in their own marriage. Moreover, dissatisfied with her earlier remarks, she recalls that "He made me get up again." She said, "I was furious!" If nothing more, this thoughtless treatment of his wife was evidence of excessive and misguided zeal. At worst, it may have been manipulative—an attempt to lure Rose Marie into committing herself verbally to things that he wanted her to do. Given its best face, which I am inclined to do, Jack may have thought that Rose Marie had more to offer than she believed. But all of this is speculation about motives that even the couple themselves might have been hard put to sort out at the time. The fact is, however, that there was great tension in their lives which eventuated in such actions and outcomes toward one another.[2]

From what I read, the pair were torn as to where, when and how Jack should carry on his ministry. They did not seem to agree even on what sort of ministry it was to which Jack was called. Should he be teaching, pastoring, planting churches,

---

taking her along with him as he did so. But Rose Marie resisted. Can you imagine Rose Marie upstairs, while Jack is witnessing to skiers below, reading Agatha Christie and praying that the money would not come in so that Jack could not hold any more "Ski and Skeptic" meetings? According to Jack, that is exactly what happened (*Manual*, 3-2).

[1] *Manual*, 2-7.

[2] Perhaps much of the tension issued from Rose Marie's claim that when Jack entered the ministry there "wasn't anything we agreed on together" concerning that decision. Evidently, it was all Jack's decision, and Rose Marie was expected to go along with it (*Manual*, 5-2).

going into missionary work—or what? Again, it seems that Jack's quest for a ministry that offered *something more* drove him from one thing to another. How much this dissatisfaction had to do with the desire for something more and how much the desire itself contributed to the dissatisfaction is difficult to say. Doubtless, once the cycle had begun, the one fed the other in a chicken-and-egg process. One thing is certain—the quest went on. It went on until, in Sonship doctrines, Jack and Rose Marie at last found that *something* for which he (and eventually she) had been looking.

As we have seen, the early uncertainty drove Jack. Others, who shared Jack's enthusiasm for evangelism and ministry in general, appreciated this early emphasis and soon began to follow him. Initially many gathered in the New Life[1] churches. But according to the Millers' testimony, all still was not going well. That *something more* was still out there somewhere beckoning him onward.

Finally in the "insights" that resulted in Sonship, Jack was able to "discover" what the rest of us apparently lacked—a new understanding of the all-pervasiveness of the gospel. In this understanding, aided by an interpretation of Luther in his early writings, Jack came to see how his new view of the gospel was the answer to his quest. This view, however, meant that he would depart from the "mere" assertion that justification was by faith. Indeed, now he would assert that sanctification was also by faith repeatedly placed in the gospel. I shall have more to say about this at a later point.

For now, it is important to observe that this new view focuses on *sanctification* which all along had been at the heart of the quest. The driving force of Jack's concern was the same as that which leads people to adopt doctrines of a "second blessing" and similar beliefs. It is the desire to find a satisfying way of life that

---

[1] This name itself demonstrated both the dissatisfaction I have been discussing and the desire for something new.

transcends that of struggling every day with our sin in a sinful world. It was a quest for a "higher life," one filled with the Spirit, that would bring the sort of joy and peace that Jack never knew. And, because that is what we all want to possess (and especially because it was presented in simple terms that required following an easily understood formula), Sonship™ appeals to those who similarly want to honor God by a greater[1] knowledge of Him and His ways.

Well, that, in a nutshell, is how I see it. Yet, the real question is whether or not the quest led to a false solution to the problem. In my opinion, it most certainly did. And, as I shall attempt to show, it deceives and fails to satisfy the basic longing[2] driving the search behind it because it is unbiblical.

---

[1] The word used by Sonship™ is "deeper," a term found in many "higher life" efforts. Reformed thinking has always avoided the higher life emphasis which tends to parcel out believers into separate categories. I shall attempt later to show you that there has been good reason for avoiding all such thinking.

[2] This seems evident from the way in which Sonshippers are taught to flagellate themselves through a life of constant and repeated repentance. The *Sonship Manual*, for instance, explains that "leaders are meant to be the *chief repenters*" (Introduction, p. iii). Repentance, rather than spontaneous upon occasions when needed, seems almost to be ritualized into a technique for attaining the ends of Sonship™. Incidentally, Sonship™ has trademarked the biblical term—hence, the ™ in the name.

Chapter Three

Experiential Orientation

It doesn't take a genius to recognize the strong experiential orientation of the Sonship movement. The lion's share of the *Manual* consists of anecdotes—principally about Jack and Rose Marie Miller. Conclusions about doctrine again and again are drawn from their experience, rather than from careful exegesis. More often than not, it seems, the Scriptures (if cited at all) are used simply to *substantiate* these conclusions. I am not prepared to say that all of the conclusions reached are wrong; certainly not. But when teaching Christian truth, the Scriptures—not human experience—should always be up-front-and-center as the foundation for that truth.

This strong experiential orientation, found chiefly in the testimonies of the founders (some of which we visited in the previous chapter) does, however, tell us what the rough, roller coaster course that they took was (is, in the case of Rose Marie and others) like. And that view of the journey, the destination, and the points along the road should help warn the reader about what he is getting into if he opts for the Sonship™ experience. Moreover, if it shows anything, it vividly shows the uncertainty and impermanence that characterizes those who use the Bible in the inadequate manner mentioned in the previous paragraph. The way is precarious.

When considering the experiences offered by the founders of Sonship one fact stands out boldly: the *very peculiar* nature of the experiences that they relate. Is it, for instance, common for wives to pray against their husband's ministries? Is it anywhere near the norm for husbands not to confer with their wives about so momentous a decision as accepting a call to the ministry? I think not. Even most "normal," unsaved sinners rarely do such strange things. Do most people consider all they do a failure, cry for two weeks over problems in their lives, or desire to kill teenagers to whom they are trying to witness?[1] There is definitely something *peculiar*—to use the least pejorative term possible— about the lives of the founders of Sonship. Indeed, looking at this rocky path that they tell us they trod on, one might almost want to call them flounders rather than founders. The word "flounder" comes to mind in relationship to Sonship not merely as a takeoff on the word founder, but because it so aptly describes the manner in which Jack and Rose Marie reached the conclusions that led to Sonship. And from viewing the record, I am afraid that they never did get beyond the floundering stage. That others have found the system unsteady as well certainly is further confirmation of the fact that for all its talk about Sonship bringing joy and peace, it offers them only a life of continual introspection,[2] wrong turns, crisis experiences and repentance.[3]

We are dealing with a couple of people who in very intensive ways struggled for meaning and peace in their lives. One was more ambitious than the other. But it seems that they didn't know how to deal with one another, talk through their problems or reach truly biblical solutions to them. The resultant doctrines upon which they uneasily came to rest reflect the great unrest and uncertainty of the search that preceded.

The problem is this: the movement has tendencies born from this struggle that are peculiar to the Millers, that they have gen-

---

[1] See *Infra.*

[2] At the conclusion of every lesson in the *Manual*, introspective questions are propounded.

[3] Interestingly enough, I was just interrupted by a phone call from the discerning pastor of a PCA church in New England who was inquiring about my opinion of Sonship™. When I told him that I was in the process of writing this chapter, he was delighted because, as he said, it seemed to him to be a very vague system that is out of accord with sound teaching.

eralized to everyone. In one place, Jack says, "Everyone of us must say, 'Yes, that is my experience, again and again.'"[1] After describing how one awakens in the morning saying, "I'm an orphan," Jack asks "That is the way we all live, isn't it?"[2] As a result, others are crammed into Jack's or Rose Marie's mold, molds that may or may not fit them. It seems from perusing the "lessons" found in the *Manual* that there is no place for anyone who doesn't fit. So the founders' experiences (together with a lesser number of their disciples' experiences) are made the norm for everyone. All must flounder their way along as did Jack and Rose Marie. One can only question the thinking that leads to so distorted an outcome.

The danger in making the peculiarities of a highly volatile couple of sinners the norm for others is that those who follow in their steps find it necessary to reproduce in their own lives the turmoil and tensions that the Millers experienced. Much (possibly most) of this effort to reproduce similar experiences is likely to lead to posturing and pretending. Disciples will (by the assignments given in the *Manual* are *encouraged* to) do so. But if they have any discernment at all, they will soon find that this feigning of lifestyles, in an attempt to fit the Miller pattern, fails to reflect the actual contours of their own peculiar problems. Certainly there are commonalities. But there are also many differences. If these differences did not exist, the Scriptures, which deal with all of human difficulties, would not have to be so voluminous. A few pages of Bible—with questions at the end of each chapter—would suffice.

The group sessions, and sessions with prayer partners, train disciples to "peel the layers of the onion" so as to bring about a desired recognition of sin and problems lying "deep" within.

---

[1] *Manual*, 6-3.

[2] *Manual*, 6-5. Posing this in the form of a question may indicate that even he had some doubt about the universality of that morning response. Certainly, most of us would find it atypical.

"Deep" is a word that pervades Sonship literature. However here, as in the terminology of Freudian "depth" psychology, however, one must question how deep the person who speaks about it really goes. A number of those who have been exposed to Sonship have commented on its superficiality. They speak of it as an instrument with only one string!

The introspection that is encouraged is said to come about "as we open our hearts" to God so as to "grow in our awareness of sin, inadequacy, weakness and inability."[1] Supposedly, "Like an onion," God "peels more and more layers of our hearts open and exposes us."[2] This process is designed to reveal the "deeper issues of pride, unbelief, self-reliance, and self-righteousness." The questions at the conclusion of the lessons in the *Manual* encourage the disciple to "share" his problems and sins with others in the group.[3] Where is the biblical basis for any such activity? Psychology has a lot to say about "group therapy;" but the concept is not recommended in the Scriptures.[4] Where churches have tried it, one of the serious problems they have found is that gossip and slander are either encouraged or allowed. If the testimonies in the *Manual* are any indication of what goes on in the groups, then people are clearly being encouraged to talk about others (children, spouses, etc.) in negative ways. Sonshippers should do some serious study of James 4:11 and kindred pas-

---

[1] *Manual*, 10-22. It is the Scripture, not some ritual of "opening" that penetrates to the depths of the heart (Hebrews 4:12, 13). Though adherents will probably say otherwise, I can only conclude that in Sonship there is little emphasis on the place of the Bible in dealing with the sin in our lives.

[2] Ibid.

[3] One really sadly unbiblical rule given is to *not* reveal to one's spouse "anything personal" that is revealed to group members (*Manual*, Introduction, p.ix). This rule indicates an unhealthy emphasis on the supreme importance given to the movement; it strongly suggests that Sonship is held more highly than one's marriage!

[4] See Appendix for a consideration of such group activity.

sages in Proverbs in relation to their group practices. God forbids all such negative speaking of others.

Moreover, the questions at the conclusion of each lesson *suggest* attitudes and behaviors that may not have existed until Sonship raised them as "issues." People may easily imagine they have problems like those suggested so as to conform to expectations set forth in the book. Examples of these questions may be found throughout the *Manual*.

When I say that these lessons and the "system" (if such conglomerate confusion can properly be so called) that they represent originated from self-confessed problem people whose experiences are atypical, I mean just that. For instance, how many of you having been "filled with joy" and having just "dedicated" a "tenth" of your life to "reaching out to people" would approach some teenage motorcycle gang members only to find yourself thinking that "There were moments that I wanted to kill one or two of those teenagers?"[1] Well, that was how Jack says *his* thinking went. One wonders from this revelation, along with all of the others, how he could dare make his experience the norm upon which to build a movement. Yet, throughout the Sonship literature Jack and Rose Marie persist in telling us not what God said but what Jack calls "my story."[2] And, frankly, the story is so strange that it sounds almost artificial and contrived at points.

What do I mean by that? Well, let's consider Rose Marie's testimony for a moment. She speaks continually about crisis moments in which "the dam. . . burst," or she "sobbed and sobbed."[3] Then there are the high points in which she supposedly found joy and peace. Jack is a crisis-oriented person as well; he seems always to be having emotional, existential

---

[1] *Manual*, 4-9.

[2] *Manual*, 4-3. Frankly, I became weary of hearing about Jack and Rose Marie as I read. I wonder if anyone else has had the same experience.

[3] *Manual*, 2-7.

moments in which he is "dumbfounded," "astonished," "amazed" and "stunned" by various insights. Yet, this sort of thing must be repeated over and over again.[1] The insights never seem to stick. They do not represent real growth. In fact, at one place Puritan Thomas Brooks is quoted favorably as saying, "Christ in this life will not free any believer from the presence of any one sin, though he doth free every believer from the damning power of every sin."[2]

Something is wrong here. Either these stupendous moments did something extraordinary for the founders as they moved out from them or they didn't—or, perhaps, there is a bit too much exaggeration in the way their stories are presented. This continual roller coaster lifestyle is certainly one that I would recommend to no one. After all, these were supposedly moments of landmark change, moments when great insights into what the gospel could do for them were enjoyed. Yet, they had to be repeated over and over again. Little, if any progress—as Brooks says—is made in overcoming sin.

This apparent hype about happenings is further illustrated by the way in which Jack represents his ministry. Whenever something right happens in his life, he is likely to tell us that, as a result, great things happened in his church,[3] on the mission field, or at the seminary. I have no way to verify or disprove the accounts of other happenings to which he refers, but I know something of the seminary. At one point Jack came back repentant to his church and to the seminary that he had earlier left in a

---

[1] Manual, 4-3, 4.

[2] *Manual,* 3-13,14. One wonders about those Christians in Corinth who are said to have put various sins behind them by the cleansing power of the Word and the Spirit (see I Corinthians 6:9-11). Can Brooks possibly mean that a drunkard must always be a drunkard? The very idea is foreign to the biblical notion of freedom from sin. No wonder, in espousing such discouraging views, the Millers seem never to get on top of their problems.

[3] *Manual,* 4-3.

huff. He claims that his return ultimately led to "the beginnings of revival, both in the seminary and in the church."[1] He speaks also of some students making "somewhat of a conversion.[2]" What does that mean? Given the vagueness of Sonship teaching, it is hard to tell. Now, there was no revival at the seminary when I was a professor. Nor do I believe that there was one after I left. I retained rather close contact with some of the faculty members and twice a year returned to teach courses. I am sure I would have heard of this revival if it had been of any significance at all. I am not accusing Jack of lying, but as he looked at things through the lens of his great desire to attain that *something more* of which I have spoken, I believe that he tended to see things in a light that others didn't. This, it seems, led to a certain hype or exaggeration.

Tying in with this experiential orientation in Sonship, the movement gives ample evidence of an overemphasis on feelings. Again and again we are treated to emotional outbursts, as you have seen. But more than that, the principle and practice of "opening" is enmeshed in feelings as well. Listen to this: "I begin to know more and more in my feeling life, in the very depths of my soul, what Christ has done for me in love."[3] Placing this statement in conjunction with the many statements that speak of Sonship helping others to live in a "deeper" way indicates that what Jack had in mind by this deeper life is some sort of inner feeling. It is certainly a matter of debate whether the feelings are the deepest level in a human being's life. Indeed, feelings are usually considered by those who are biblically-oriented as the more superficial level of life. Listening to the story of Jack and Rose Marie, however, shows how much they operated according to feelings, impressions, and the like. No wonder

---

[1] *Manual,* 11-10
[2] Whatever that means! *Manual,* 11-9.
[3] *Manual,* 3-6.

it was a roller coaster ride! The road paved with feelings is a bumpy and dangerous course to follow.

The crisis-filled, roller coaster lives of which we read in the *Manual* give evidence of two people who, whether consciously or not, were dominated by feelings. The insights that they supposedly received (always attached to great emotional surges) were never enough to satisfy. They found, instead, that they had to go from one emotional experience to another, much like the priest who offers a daily sacrifice in the temple that can never take away sin. The once for all (*hapax*) of the sacrifice, in contrast, seems to be missing.

In 1975 Rose Marie said, "Into my life came a new freedom and deep joy."[1] It must have been fleeting because four years later in 1979 she records how she was still resisting Jack's ministry in Uganda, saying such things as, "Jack, you do your thing, let me do mine." Then, in Zurich, once again she experienced "deep forgiveness and joy." Up and down. Up and down. Repentance after repentance. That is the Sonship™ experience![2] The words of Thomas Brooks were well quoted as a description of it. Should we encourage others to get on this experiential roller coaster? I think not.

---

[1] Quotations in this paragraph are from *Manual*, 2-6; 2-7
[2] It reminds me of those who come forward in "altar calls" over and over again to rededicate their lives.

Chapter Four

Vague Language and Questionable Ideas

The most frequent comment I have heard from those who have had contact with Sonship and come away unimpressed is that "It's vague." The pastor who phoned me yesterday again voiced that concern. As I see it, there are several reasons why this assessment is made. First, the Millers don't seem to be systematic thinkers. That, of course, fits in with their disjointed lives. As the woman in Atlanta who listened to their tapes said, "they ramble." Presenting their message in testimonial form tends not to lead to consistency or order. The writings of their followers seem to be more academically influenced; thus their chapters in the *Manual* are more didactic.

Moreover, the Millers' speeches are shot through with stories and events that take a disproportionate amount of the speech to tell. That leaves little time or space for exposition. Information is imparted—whenever it is—through creating and leaving impressions more than through analysis and careful interpretation of events. Furthermore, apart from a few large concepts, there is little defining vocabulary. The words "orphan" and "servant"[1] are opposed to "sons." That set of words remains consistent. And the phrase "Preach the gospel to yourself," an act that is supposed to lead to "repentance," is fairly consistently used. But apart from those and a few other words and phrases, there is little technical vocabulary.

---

[1] Biblically, "servant" is a positive term. See *Manual*, 6-6.

In addition, there is the problem of loose language. (If the reader thinks that the language is precise, then we must charge the Millers with loose theology. I prefer to think that they simply were careless in the use of certain terms.) In at least three places, for instance, we encounter the word "miracle." Once it refers to the healing of a boy who was shot in the eye with a BB gun.[1] In another place Jack says that when he gave Rose Marie Luther's commentary on Galatians he "didn't interpret it to her." He then comments, "That's a miracle right there!" Further, Jack speaks of his asking Rose Marie on one occasion to pray for him as a miracle.[2] Then, two pages later he says, "The glory comes down when this person sees a miracle."

A miracle is not the healing of an eye; it is the growing of a new eye in the place of one that has been gouged out. It is not the restraint of one's usual forwardness in speech or even saying the right thing on occasion; it is speaking in a foreign language that you have never studied. The occasions cited may be classified properly as the good hand of God in providence, but not as miracles. "Why make a fuss over this use of language? Aren't you being picky? Are you *looking* for things that might be wrong?" No, that isn't the way to critique a book. But, remember, this is a book in which Jack and others attempt to straighten out people's erroneous thoughts and ways by pointing out the true path. It sets itself up as explaining a new way of life that is superior to and more biblical than the old one that most of us follow. It therefore ought to be precise. The fact is, in a day in which so many out there are fraudulently claiming to perform miracles, a person who is careful about his language will not use this term loosely.

The very fact that Jack and Paul, his son, carelessly use the word miracle must give us pause about what they say about other matters. Is their language elsewhere to be trusted to mean what it says? And to boot, we cannot help asking, "How can people who

---

[1] *Manual*, 10-21.
[2] *Manual*, 11-10.

know the difference between providence and miracles (as they certainly do) ever mix the two up?" Are the Millers simply careless, or do they really want us to believe that God has strewn miracles in their path? After all, the word "miracle," when used about someone's work, tends to lend it authority. Miracles in the Bible are said to authenticate the message and the messenger (Acts 2:22; Hebrews 2:3, 4). Is that the intent in the use of this language?

The use of miracle in this imprecise manner alerts us to look more carefully at other matters. And when we do—as well as when reading through the *Manual*—we encounter all sorts of vague and uncertain language and concepts. The book is filled with statements like "drinking freely of God's love toward us"[1] without ever explaining what this means or how one does so. It is a lovely picture-phrase, but in a book in which one is supposedly being instructed in the ways of a new life there is need for more specificity. But can the Millers objectify their thoughts and experiences in precise language? Does their chaotic lifestyle also surface in this use of language? Much like the mystics who encounter a problem in speaking of their union with God, the Millers like to use phrases and expressions that convey impressions and no more. It is hard to nail down language like that in the *Manual*. Jack's undergraduate study at college was in English. He knew writing and language. Why did he choose to be imprecise? Or did he choose? Like other things, did he throw his early training to the winds?

Here is another example: "Get infected with joy! It comes out of grace!"[2] And another: "If the conscience is noisy by disobedience, you need to move out on the basis of the atonement."[3] One more of a similar sort: "Is there terrible pride

---

[1] *Manual*, Introduction, p. iii.
[2] *Manual*, 1-7.
[3] *Manual*, 3-9.

keeping you from drinking in grace. . . ?"[1] Jack is writing like a
poet rather than like an instructor.

Rose Marie has a similar problem. She keeps talking about
"the song of the gospel" which we must hear and learn to sing.[2]
But like these other expressions, this is a vague, highly subjec-
tive matter, an impressionistic word-painting that might be filled
in by every reader in his own way. It really conveys nothing specific and allows for all sorts of interpretations that may take one
far afield from what she has in mind. But of course we must ask,
what *does* she have in mind? Is it clear to *her*? That is a serious
question. All I can see for sure is that the word-picture merely
calls for **something more** than the church's usual understanding
of the gospel.[3]

Here is another imprecise statement that fails to communi-
cate truth, leaving the reader open to believe anything that he
subjectively thinks or feels: "God just works in the deepest part
of the heart to please Him. Then you know what pleases Him.
You just know."[4] But we *don't* "just know." Always be suspi-
cious of statements that use the word "just" in that way. They
sound like some sort of qualification is attached when none is
really given. We can find the will of God for our lives in no other
place than the Scriptures.[5] Certainly not in our hearts! The heart
of a believer retains many deceitful and evil patterns. While we
have been made new persons and have hearts with a new orientation in Christ, we are by no means perfect. There is much of the
old man still left within. The stories of Jack and Rose Marie
amply illustrate that fact. Therefore, we dare not trust our hearts,
apart from their conformity to the Scriptures, to lead us in the

---

[1] *Manual*, 4-11.
[2] *Manual*, 5-1, etc.
[3] This is a matter that we must pursue in a later chapter.
[4] *Manual*, 5-6.
[5] See my book *The Christian's Guide to Guidance*.

right direction. Once more, we encounter a dangerous subjectivism that does an end run around the Scriptures.

Take two more (I'll not bore you with too many, though I possibly could adduce enough quotations to do so): "Faith preparation, then, is to feed yourself on the gospel. . . ."[1] That sounds great; but what does it mean? How is it done? What is the corresponding biblical injunction? In attempting to define faith, Paul Miller concludes that "FAITH IS JESUS"[2] (the capitals are his, showing how important a concept he thinks this is). The fact is that his statement simply isn't true—even in some metaphorical sense. It is confusing, to say the least. But it is typical of the vague, ill-defined nature of Sonship teaching. Striking phrases like this are worse than useless, if they convey an inaccurate thought. How can one be instructed well by mysticism, feeling-oriented ways, or sheer confusion of language, when there is no clue as to how to apply such statements in a practical way? And, remember, this course is oriented toward people who need help. I suppose the answer to my queries will be that there is a leader who can explain to his group what the Millers have in mind. But why not make it clear in the first place? And we must certainly ask, how much clearer are the leaders themselves when they have been trained by the very people who gave these speeches?

There is one other problem of this nature that echoes through the pages of the *Manual*. It has to do with guidance and special revelation. But because this is so important a matter, I shall reserve my comments about it for the next chapter. Suffice it to say that one wonders what it is that disciples are instructed to believe and do when they are introduced to Sonship. I think that there must be almost as many ideas of what Sonship is as there are disciples. Certainly, viewing it simply as an instruction manual for those who are confused and sinning, we can say that the

---

[1] *Manual*, 6-11. How does one "feed" on the gospel? And, incidentally, where do we read any such thing in the Word of God?

[2] *Manual*, 9-4.

book offers warm fuzzies, but does precious little to instruct in the ways of God found in the Scriptures. Sinful people don't need confused, confusing material that only adds to their own confusion. They need clarity and precision, traits that do not characterize the speeches and the writings we find in the *Manual*.

Chapter Five

Scripture, Subsequent Revelation, and Guidance

One of the more serious difficulties with Sonship teaching is that it takes its stand with those who believe that it is still possible to obtain special revelation from God in addition to the Scriptures. This extra-biblical revelation supposedly takes place in reliance upon circumstances, sensings of God's presence, spiritual "nudgings," and—of greater significance—explicit statements that the Spirit spoke (usually to Rose Marie[1]). These communications, supposedly from the Spirit, are placed in quotation marks.

If indeed the Spirit spoke, as is claimed, we had better copy His statements into our Bibles. They would be every bit as valid revelations as those that we now have in the Scriptures. And, as a matter of fact, since they were given in our time and in our culture, it is likely that they would be of even greater value to us!

Let's take a look at some of the things that are said in this regard. At the outset, journaling is encouraged. We read, "Set a time once a day or once a week to write in your journal. Facilitate this by having times where you are silent and seeking to listen to what God wants to teach you. Then just start writing. Jot down anything."[2] If they had suggested that this exercise was

---

[1] Though Paul Miller also speaks of the Spirit "touching" him and he hearing "His voice" (Manual, 12-4).

[2] *Manual*, Introduction, p. viii.

one in which you would write out what you have learned in the Scriptures about your life—that might be OK. But to add the words about being "silent and seeking to listen to what God wants to teach you" takes quite a different turn. We are not told how it is that God is supposed to speak, but it is clear that some sort of communication is to be expected from Him. This is not simply "loose language." After all, why be "silent" and "listen" if there is nothing to hear? In accord with what we have already learned about Sonship, this practice fits into the supposedly "superior" nature of the movement. Here is a group whose goal is to connect you to a special pipeline from God, by which you can learn His will for you by sitting quietly and listening. That is something that the rest of us peons cannot do. But where do the Scriptures teach any such thing? The fact is, they do not. Special revelation through journaling is a very dangerous elitist doctrine. The dangers lie in the fact that one opens himself to any and all influences. There is no assurance that what he "hears" will be from God. On the contrary, since the canon is closed we can be certain that it will not be from God.

The assigned journaling is a dominant part of the Sonship discipling program. Following every lesson, the student is asked if he did his journaling. He indicates that he has by checking off a box. Do you suppose that it is in the quiet moments when God is supposed to speak that He reveals the meanings of those vague ideas mentioned in the previous chapter? No wonder the Scriptures are neglected in this movement! If I could get special revelation by journaling, I'd neglect them too. After all, the revelation of the will of God obtained in this way is immediate, personal, directed to the present situation and (presumably) in English rather than Greek, Aramaic or Hebrew! In fact, if I could learn from God this way every day as I quietly sit, that method would regularly supplant the study of the Bible for me.

But it is not only during the time when one is journaling that revelation is said to be given. During a communion service, Rose

Marie recounts, "When Jack broke the bread, the Spirit said to me, 'I was the one who took that spear and broke the side of Jesus because of my sins of self-righteousness, deep self-centeredness, of thinking that there is life to be lived apart from God.'"[1] Apart from the doctrinal issues involved in the supposed revelation of the Spirit's spearing of the Savior, notice what we have here: this is a very personal application of a biblical passage that goes beyond[2] the passage itself. But even the application doesn't fit the facts. Since the spear was thrust into Jesus only after His death, what the "revelation" says is incorrect. Christ, the *living* Savior, *"died"* for our sins. It was not a corpse that was punctured by a spear for our sins (John 19:33, 34)! When Jesus said, "It is finished" (John 19:30) He had already completed His sacrificial work on the cross. So here we have teaching supposedly from the Spirit that contradicts the Bible! If that is what we can expect from the founders of this movement, all I can say is "Why bother to study Sonship?"

In another place, Rose Marie again quotes the Holy Spirit: "Then finally the Spirit was teaching me, 'Rose Marie in spite of all your sin and her [daughter's] sin, this really is the work of the enemy. He really did this and now let's pray against that work.'"[3] I will not comment on the way in which this supposed revelation got her "off the hook." All I can say is that if this sort of thing really happens and is not merely a figment of our imagination, then most Christians in the history of the church have been wrong and the canon is not closed.

---

[1] *Manual,* 2-5, 6. The sentence is somewhat convoluted, and obviously didn't come from the Holy Spirit. It seems to say that the Holy Spirit's sins were involved in Christ's crucifixion whereas the intent must be that Rose Marie's sins were in view. The word "my" should be "your." Perhaps, also, she is trying to say that *her* sins speared the Lord.

[2] Cf. II John 9. There is grave danger in "going beyond" the Bible.

[3] *Manual,* 5-5.

But the Spirit comes not only in communion services and in quiet times, according to Rose Marie, He also comes in times when we are talking to others: "The Spirit kept nudging me [One wonders how? What exactly is it to which she is referring?], saying, [and once again, she quotes the Spirit] 'Rose Marie, you are not through yet. You have got to say more.'"[1] This "nudging" sounds similar to what others call "promptings." I suppose that what she is referring to is some sort of inner uneasiness that she interpreted as a "nudge" to go on speaking. Yet, perhaps Rose Marie means more than this. Once again, there are the *quotation marks* that accompany the "nudge." That fact seems to say that supposedly there was some didactic element in the revelatory nudge.

In Lesson 13-8 we read more about how the Spirit supposedly works in Sonship: "The Holy Spirit comes in deep [there's that word again] conviction and he says, 'Rose Marie, here is where you live, and here is where you need the approval of men. Now, let's get rid of that and let your conscience be under God's approval.'" It is interesting that the Spirit is represented as speaking in the language of "need" theology! No one "needs" man's approval. The concept of such inner needs is a modern one that has trickled into Christianity from the writings of pagan psychologists. Scripture makes it abundantly clear that only one thing is needful (Luke 10:39, 42). There is something decidedly wrong here!

On the next page, we are assured by Rose Marie that "Our feelings will often tell us that something is wrong, but the Spirit will always tell us what the real problem is." How convenient! Don't you wish it were true? And, by the way, there is no suggestion about how one can distinguish feelings from spiritual nudgings.

---

[1] *Manual* 13-3.

In an article in the *Harvester*, which is a publication of Sonship's World Harvest Mission, Rick Gray wrote the following, which is reproduced in the *Manual* (15-23): "Jesus *is* breaking through! He has begun a fresh liberating work! The weapons of His warfare are many: His providence in my circumstances, the prayers and communion of honest saints, a godly counselor, the light of His Word, and His Spirit's voice." In this sentence, the *voice* of the Spirit is *clearly distinguished* from the Scriptures. There seems to be no doubt, then, that the movement teaches and practices the concept of continuing, personal revelation from the Holy Spirit of God. No wonder it thinks that it may make statements that are "beyond" the Bible.

There is great danger in these statements and in the practices that they describe and advocate. Nothing is said of how one may distinguish the "voice" of the Spirit (were it to be heard as they claim) from some other voice—one's own, a demon's, etc. All is left up to the disciple. Nothing could be more disconcerting to an honest, trusting sinner who wants to know God's will for his life than to attempt to discern the voice of God in a quiet time or in some other situation, only to find that he hears *nothing*. Moreover, if he thinks that possibly he is being "nudged," he may not be certain and may not know whether to act on the impulse or not. Sonship leads him up a tree, out on a limb—and leaves him there!

Plainly, the movement has incorporated elements that distinguish it from classical Reformed thinking. So long as it holds to extra-biblical revelation, Sonship can never fairly substantiate the claim that theologically it is no different from other Reformed groups. Nothing could be more dangerous to any movement than to cut itself loose from the Bible in favor of supposed additional revelation.

I can hear it now: "But we use the Bible." You can't tell me that the Bible is as significant as current, on-the-spot guidance from the Spirit—if that were actually available! Perhaps this is the most serious problem in Sonship. But, if not, it surely vies in importance with Sonship's view of the central truth of the Christian faith—its view of the gospel. We shall now look at what Sonship teaches about the cross and its meaning in the life of the believer.

Chapter Six

What is True Sonship?

The heart of the problem with Sonship™ lies in its concept of sonship.[1] And that is related directly to its view of the gospel. The interrelation of these two factors is uppermost in the teachings of this group. According to Sonship, the problem with most Christians is that they are living as if they were orphans rather than as sons. They are living as if they had never been adopted into the heavenly family. Because of this, they fail to appreciate and appropriate the rights and privileges granted to them by their heavenly Father. That is why they do not grow spiritually, lead powerless and miserable lives, and are ineffective as believers. Sonship claims that the answer to all such problems is to revisit the fact of one's adoption. It is to realize afresh the meaning of the gospel. In this way, the gospel is what changes and empowers a Christian throughout life.

How is this done? It is done by preaching the gospel to one's self over and over again and by "practic[ing] every day believing the gospel."[2] This continued experience begins by repentance. One repents of sins, but principally of the sin of failing to recognize and appropriate his sonship.

What's wrong with that? Well, a number of things that I shall mention in this chapter. But to sum up, we may say that Sonship

---

[1] Not to say that the other matters already reviewed are not of great moment. But Sonship makes much of the idea of sonship and incessantly drums into the disciple that he needs to repent and once more believe the gospel which he is encouraged to preach again and again to himself.

[2] *Manual*, 7-11.

makes too much of adoption (sonship) in some respects and, at the same time, makes too little of it in other respects.

The Greek word *huiothesia* (found in Galatians 4:5) means "son-placing" or "adoption." It is a legal term that defines the status of an individual before the law.[1] It declares that the heavenly Father has received a believer into the position of full sonship in the heavenly family. To him, all the rights and privileges of sonship have been granted. This is a wonderful fact that takes place when one is "justified by faith." In this act, he is counted (reckoned) perfect on the books of heaven because all of the righteousness of Christ in fulfilling the law is attributed to him as if *he* had done it. Remember, however, that the transaction is in every sense a *legal* one.

The problem with Sonship™ is that it misidentifies the source of sanctification (or the fruitful life of the children of God) as justification. Justification, though a wonderful fact, a ground of assurance, and something never to forget, cannot produce a holy life though a strong motive for it,. As a declaration of forgiveness, pardon, and adoption into the family of God, it is (remember) a *legal* act. It changes the standing, but not the condition, of the person who is justified.

On the other hand, *regeneration* (quickening, or making alive; Ephesians 2:5) is the true source of sanctification. Justification deals with guilt; regeneration and sanctification deal with corruption. Regeneration, the true source of sanctification (growing out of sinful living into holy living), provides spiritual life to believe the gospel together with new capability to resist sin, and to obey God's commandments through the Holy Spirit, Whose coming Christians have been "created in Christ Jesus for good works." All of this is all of grace, making the believer nothing less than God's handiwork (Ephesians 2:10).

---

[1] *Huios,* the first half of the compound word *huiothesia,* is the legal term for "son."

One is not able to do works of righteousness by means of his own wisdom or in his own strength. The continued work of the Spirit provides that wisdom and strength so as to enable the Christian to obey. This He does through the instrumentality of the book that is peculiarly His—the Bible (cf. Romans 15:13, 4; note how those things promised in verse 13 are said in verse 4 to accrue to the Christian through the Scriptures). These works that please God are the fruit (result of the inner working) of the Spirit.

Thus, all of the things that the "natural person" could not achieve (I Corinthians 2:6-16), the regenerated person is now capable of doing by the Spirit. It is the Spirit, for instance, Who makes love—the summary of the law, according to Christ—possible (Romans 5:5). The Spirit within wars against the flesh (old thoughts and ways that were developed by the pre-regenerate sinful nature), and as He wins more and more battles His "fruit" becomes more and more evident in the Christian.

Though the Spirit produces fruit, He does it through, and not apart from, human effort (which He initiates and sustains). This is clear from the fact that Christians themselves are commanded to become involved in the "pursuit of fruit"—the very same fruit that is said to be the fruit of the Spirit.[1] This pursuit is real, involving biblical study and struggles with sin that issue in failures and successes.

Moreover, not only is the Christian everywhere in the Bible exhorted to obey God's commands rather than merely repent and believe the gospel, when he fails he is dealt with as a disobedient son with whom God is thereby displeased (Revelation 3:19), who must not only repent and remember God's goodness but also (specifically) must "*do* the first works" (Revelation 2:5). If he fails to do so, all of the preaching of the gospel to himself

---

[1] See my book *The Christian Counselor's Manual* pp. 250ff. for details about this matter.

again (a non-biblical concept that seems to be the slogan of Sonship) will not restore the light of God's countenance.

Plainly, the error of substituting justification for regeneration (quickening) is at the heart of the difficulty that Sonship presents to the Christian. It fails to explain what God has done for him in making him a new creation and how he may conform to the will of God. It is the new regenerate life with its new capacity to please God that enables the Spirit Who quickened him to help Him grow by His grace. The grace (help) of the Lord Jesus Christ that Paul desires for believers (Galatians 6:18, and elsewhere) is mediated through the Holy Spirit Whom He sent as a counselor like Himself to aid believers.

There is another Greek term that is used in Scriptures to describe the relationship of the believer to his heavenly Father. It is *teknon*. This word, in contrast to *huiothesia* (the forensic word that Sonship™ repeatedly emphasizes), speaks of the warm, affectionate relationship of a child to his parent. It has to do with the life relationship of the two *after* adoption. It is of significance that the legal force of the former term pervades the thinking of Sonshippers while the intent of the latter term is barely mentioned.

Sonship *wants* to go beyond the legal relationship, but has difficulty doing so because the only way it knows is to have the Christian go back to the adoption experience by preaching the gospel—justification by faith—to himself once again.[1] But that won't do it. Having four adopted children myself, I can tell you that this isn't how caring relationships are developed or grow. Rather, these are fostered by the give-and-take of the *subsequent* relationship. Revisiting the initial adoption event won't cut it! It is what follows the *huiothesia* event that builds and then "deepens" the relationship of a father to his children. How sterile (not to say futile) it would be for me to repeatedly remind my chil-

---

[1] Cf. *Manual* 4-10, 11.

dren of the fact that they were adopted (legally made my sons) as a means of helping them to obey and grow! The *legal* must be supplanted by the *actual*. What builds a loving relationship is all of the many caring times together over the years following the adoption.

Can you imagine me telling my children over and over again, "remember you were adopted, remember that I made you *legally* my child" as the means of helping them to find the joys of sonship? The idea is preposterous. They know full well whose child they are. But it is not to the adoption that they look for a solution to present problems, but to me as a parent with whom they have had a history of subsequent events that has built our relationship. My wife and I *treat* our children *as children* and, consequently, they know they are! Love, care, help of every sort through the years, are what develop true sonship. The same is true of God and His children.

Now, of course, that relationship includes discipline, something that Sonship seems to know little about. Here, too little is made of the *teknon* relationship. Indeed, in the Scriptures discipline is represented as a prominent factor in recognizing one's sonship. Listen to these verses:

> God is treating you like sons. What son is there that a father doesn't discipline? But if you are without discipline. . . then you are illegitimate children and not sons. (Hebrews 12:7, 8).

and

> I convict and discipline those about whom I care. (Revelation 3:19).

Indeed, in Sonship, there seems to be no recognition of the fact that guilty children (guilt is seen as a bad thing[1]) must seek the

---

[1] Though, inconsistently, repentance is urged. But the repentance seems to be mostly about considering one's self an orphan rather than a son.

forgiveness of their heavenly Father as well as of their siblings in the Lord. Sonship seems to have forgotten the words of the *Westminster Confession of Faith* in which we are told that Fatherly discipline grows out of "Fatherly displeasure" whereby the sinning believer loses "the light of His countenance" until he humbles himself in repentance (W.C.F. XIII:5; cf. also Matthew 6:12, 14, 15). Chastisement is intended to bring guilty children to repentance about whatever sins they may have committed.

Because the life of true sonship is all but absent from Sonship, Sonshippers seem to address guilt only from the perspective of God as *Judge*. (Once again, the legal or forensic emphasis seems uppermost.) There is a lack of understanding of the guilt that comes from disobeying God as a heavenly *Father*, and of the family discipline that follows. God is pictured almost as an indulgent Father Who spoils His children by failing to chastise them because he adopted them. The words in I Corinthians 11:29-32, indicating how God treats erring, unrepentant children, should dispel any such soft views.

Since in Sonship the focus is on the past (the legal adoption as sons), the present is sadly neglected. From an effort to avoid legalism and works-righteousness, a new legalism has emerged. This legalism stresses a prescribed ritual of preaching of the gospel over and over again to one's self rather than teaching the ways of biblical, filial obedience. Little or nothing appears in the literature about obedience. A person becomes bound by the ever-occurring ritual of self-confrontation in preaching rather than being freed to live for Christ by learning God's ways and keeping His commandments.

Progress and true growth seem impossible in Sonship. (Indeed, as noted on page 18, Thomas Brooks is quoted favorably as teaching "Christ in this life will not free the believer from the presence of any one sin.")[1] The progress that is encour-

---

[1] This teaching seems to ignore such passages as I Corinthians 6:9-11 where sinners of all sorts are said to have been able to put these sins behind them by

aged throughout the Bible is stifled by Sonship's unbiblical insistence on always going back to the beginning.[1] On the contrary, in Hebrews 6:1, "maturity" is envisioned as *leaving* the "elementary principles" and *going on,* or *advancing,* to other things. Indeed, the writer of Hebrews is at cross purposes with Sonship. Rather than going on to maturity, the Sonshipper is taught to return to infancy.

Growth, according to Sonship, means taking the backward look, rehearsing over and over again that one has been made a son. Hebrews, instead, tells us that growth comes from moving on, "not laying the foundation" again. It comes from learning new truths from the Scriptures and, by faith and power and wisdom of the Spirit, putting them into practice. There is much talk about faith among Sonshippers, but little or no talk of the works that James says will follow true faith.[2]

Consequently, as the writer of Hebrews says, Sonshippers seem to have become "dull in hearing" (5:11-12). When they "ought to be teachers" they need to hear the "elementary principles of God's revelation once again." The counsel they give is to prefer the "milk" of the Word over "solid food."

---

the sanctifying power of the Holy Spirit: "Such *were* some of you." Some Puritanism was quite unbiblical. Too many Christians uncritically accept whatever any Puritan writer has to say. Does a drunkard or adulterer have no hope of ever changing his ways? The heart of our faith is that God can make us new in Christ, enabling us to live in ways that please God.

[1] A true father wants to see his son grow and mature. He helps him to do so at every turn. In Sonship™ God teaches little that spurs on growth. Instead, He takes his son back to the basics again and again. A son learns how to hammer and saw; but never how to use those skills, once learned, to build anything. Indeed, it is a fair question whether Sonshippers believe that one may ever reach a stage of maturity where, in this life, he may please God by building a life for Him.

[2] The church that had fallen from its heights was exhorted not to preach the gospel to itself again, but to "do" its "first works"! Clearly, there is a different emphasis here.

Why is this? Hebrews 5:13-14 explains:

> The truth is that everyone who feeds on milk is inexperienced with the righteous Word; he is still a baby. Solid food is for mature people, for those whose faculties have been trained by practice to distinguish good from evil.

The Sonship movement gives every evidence of a superficial understanding of the Word of God. When Scripture is used, too often that use is non-exegetical.[1] Rather, Scripture is made to support the experience-derived theories upon which Sonship is actually based. Listen to this: "Christ meets me at the point of failure. In fact, that is often the only place he meets me. This is when I'm doing my best"[2] (*Manual*, 8-17). That statement is simply not true about believers. Christ regularly confronts obedient, growing Christians in the Bible when they are failures—or not.[3]

Joseph Smith, the founder of Mormonism, claimed to have retranslated portions of the Bible so as to restore "plain and precious promises" that had been lost or distorted. In Hebrews 6:1, without any manuscript authority whatsoever, he added the word

---

[1] Many sentences in the *Manual* contain mere affirmations that begin with such words as "I think, I believe" rather than "God says" (followed by exegetical support). Though they would strenuously deny it, I suppose, the final authority in Sonship is experience—especially the experiences of the Millers.

[2] Note the gloomy note toward any human effort that is sounded in this last statement.

[3] As far as I can tell, only Tim Keller, in his *Galatians: New Freedom, New Family* (version 3.1) attempts to justify the notion that growth in Christian living comes through preaching the gospel to one's self (p. 4). The verse he keys on is Colossians 1:6 in which he sees the gospel as "a living thing" that grows "in us and renew[s] us" (Week 7, p. 2). However, the growth of which Paul writes has to do with the spread of the gospel among the Colossians and throughout the whole world. The passage is not speaking of our growth as believers.

"not" so that the verse in his so-called *Inspired Translation* reads, "not leaving the elementary teachings about Christ." He entirely misrepresented the writer's intent. While Sonshippers have not added a word to the inspired record so as to reverse its meaning as Smith did, their practice of reverting to the elementary teaching of legal adoption amounts to much the same thing.

Certainly all of us may frequently look back to the time when we became sons and rejoice in the fact, but there is no directive to do so for growth, or even an example of this practice, in the New Testament. And surely there is nothing to support the ritual act of repeatedly doing so as a *technique* of growth! Something so prominent as the prime practice in the Sonship movement ought to have a correspondingly prominent place in the Bible. The true reminder of the good news about Jesus' death for our sins is the one that He left for us to observe—the Lord's supper ("Do this in remembrance of Me").

How is it that Sonship has come to its beliefs? Peter explains: "Unstable and untaught persons. . . twist the Scriptures" (II Peter 3:16). Jack Miller was not untaught (or even ill-taught), but it seems that in time he rejected much of what he was taught, replacing it with self-taught ideas.[1] It is clear from the record that he and Rose Marie have left us that he was unstable.

As I have pointed out, Sonship is the attempt to get something more (for example, to "feel God's presence"[2]). The trag-

---

[1] In response to a letter from someone who accused Jack of insulting "2000 years of church history," Jack wrote "Listen, without grace, 2000 years of church history is insulting to God" (*Manual,* 3-5). Of course, his statement is literally true. But, doubtless, this man was also taking issue with Jack's questionable view of grace. The idea that most have been wrong about grace in sanctification is a tenet of Sonship.

[2] *Manual,* 6-16. Of course, it is impossible to "feel or sense God's presence" since He is a Spirit and does not have a body. This language gives further evidence of the loose thinking and expressions that Sonshippers use to describe emotional experiences that the Millers sought and produced.

edy is that in the pursuit of this goal, Sonshippers embrace not
only something *more* but something *else*—something *different*.
That is what is biblically unsound about Sonship teaching. The
principal problem, then, is how Sonship links justification to
sanctification. Like other wrong systems of sanctification, Sonship postulates *something more* than does the historic position.
That is what Jack was looking for and that is exactly what he
found. People often seem to "find" what they seek—one way or
another!

Sanctification is said to take place by faith alone as justification does. Any effort on the part of the Christian is said to be
wrong. The cooperative nature of the human and the divine in
sanctification is neglected or dismissed; Sonshippers label the
human side of sanctification as works-righteousness. The fact is
that no Reformed teacher of any note has ever taught that this
cooperative effort is works-righteousness. Rather, human effort
in the process of sanctification has always been understood as
the result of the Spirit's work in the heart, encouraging and
enabling the believer to obey God's commands. These works are
denominated, as in Galatians 5, "the Spirit's fruit." In Philippians 2:13 Paul states it clearly: "it is God Who is producing in
you both the willingness and the ability to do the things that
please Him." But note that the *believer* is the one who does
them. God does not do them *for* him or *instead* of him.

In the section of the *Manual* entitled "Vague Feelings Versus
The Truth" (8-16), we read, "The principal way that you grow is
by believing." In it, we also read "The power of bad habits is
broken at the foot of the cross. Keep going back and repenting
even if you keep doing it [the sinful habit]." Elsewhere, we are
assured by Sonship that the cross is what Christ *now* does.[1] That
is not what the Bible teaches. Indeed, the statement sounds

---

[1] This sounds almost like a variety of transubstantiation. Sonship disciples
are taught that the gospel is "the power to save you each day" (*Manual*, 9-14).

almost like the sacrifice on the cross was not a once for all[1] act. While faith is essential, it is not alone, as James says: "Faith without works is dead." Sinful habits must be replaced by their biblical alternatives as the latter are developed by the Spirit as His fruit.

Sonship ideas confuse the relation of justification to sanctification. In doing so, Sonship strays far from the Reformed camp that it claims to be associated with. What is substituted for the Reformed position (that sanctification consists of progressively putting off the old ways of unrighteousness while putting on God's new righteous ways[2]), is a pietistic quietism that sees growth as a more-or-less mysterious result of the Spirit's work in response to faith. In Sonship, the *pursuit* of fruit[3] is discouraged even though Paul urges Timothy to "pursue righteousness" and virtually all of those items mentioned as His fruit in Galatians 5 (I Timothy 6:11; II Timothy 2:22). For Sonship, the production of the fruit of the Spirit is merely a matter of faith. "Pursuing" (or hunting down) fruit, however, is a vigorous human activity. Fruit production is not a passive thing, as the Sonship people seem to think. It takes cultivation to grow fruit. Yet, apart from faith, Sonshippers virtually deny human responsibility in spiritual growth.[4]

Sonship postulates a constant return to preaching the gospel to one's self as the means of sanctification. "The cross is the

---

[1] The Greek word used for the once-for-allness of the cross is *hapax*.

[2] That is true of sanctification, but in Sonship it is said to be true of justification. Sanctification and justification seem to overlap or become confused in Sonship. The fact is, the Spirit produces an actual righteousness in a believer that increasingly, though never perfectly, begins to approximate that which is attributed to him in justification.

[3] See my books *A Theology of Christian Counseling*, Chapter 15, and *The Delicate Balance*, Chapters 12 and 21, for a detailed discussion of this matter.

[4] Scripture and obedience get short shrift in Sonship. We are told that there are but "two weapons" in the struggle with sin: "one is the gospel and the other is prayer. . . there isn't anything else" (*Manual*, 6-3).

ongoing power of the Christian life" (*Manual*, 8-16). In the process, the gospel is said to have the power to sanctify. There is no
such teaching in the Bible.[1] How can "good news" (the meaning
of the word "gospel") have such power? That it is *the power of
God* unto salvation (Romans 1:16) we know is true; and that it is
the message that, believed, justifies. That makes sense. But sanctification involves the alteration of one's lifestyle, which does
not occur through believing the good news. News doesn't exert
some magical power over a person. It may have informative and
persuasive power, of course. But it cannot of itself (even through
faith) alter a person's lifestyle. Moreover, of greatest significance, in Scripture it is never said to have such power. The gospel tells of God's once-for-all[2] saving work on our behalf, and
that may beget gratitude which, in turn, convinces us to love
more fully and serve more faithfully. But the message itself has
no power to direct or enable us to carry out those good inten-
tions.

The power that we need, and that we received as Christians,
as we saw in Philippians 2:13, is found only in the person and
work of the Holy Spirit. He was given to us to effect regeneration ("quickening") and to enable us to believe the good news
and subsequently observe all that Christ has commanded us
(Matthew 28:20). The fruit that becomes evident in the life of a

---

[1] We are even told strange things such as the "gospel is empowered" by
prayer (*Manual,* 6-3). One of the chief difficulties that we encounter in Sonship is a failure to define the gospel. Indeed, because Sonship stretches it to
cover nearly everything, it is given no definition at all. Clearly, there is a general sense given to the good news, as when we read of "the good news of the
kingdom." That is, the good news that the kingdom has come. But within that
general good news, there is a specific, detailed good news that saves. In
I Corinthians 15:1-4, Paul, who ought to know if anyone does, defined the
saving gospel as consisting of two points, both of which were according to
Old Testament prophecy. They are "that Christ died for our sins" and that,
having been buried, "He was raised on the third day."
[2] Hebrews 10:10-12.

true believer is called His fruit because it is He Who by His internal working enables us to produce it.

Justification is a wonderful, judicial declaration that ought to inspire profound gratitude; but apart from human action, motivated by that gratitude, it can do nothing in and of itself to sanctify. A declaration has no power to do that. It is a fact, not a force. Justification brings peace to the troubled, fearful soul since by it we are declared righteous in God's sight (Romans 5:1). It assures us that God is for us rather than against us and that He has adopted us rather than disowned us. In it all, there is no merit in us; justification is grounded solely on the work of Christ. Similarly, since the fruit of the Spirit is due entirely to the enabling of the Spirit, there is no merit in a Christian's works. Grace is behind justification and sanctification alike.

Children, even adopted ones, are treated fully as children and therefore are expected to obey their Father. Obedience by a believer is another way to express what James refers to as "good works." Without such works, one's faith is, at best, suspect. So, let us be sure that we are not led astray by any teaching that would demean godly obedience. We must ever distinguish the relation of justification to sanctification from the relation of regeneration (quickening) to sanctification (a line we have seen seriously blurred in Sonship teaching). Only then will we be able to enjoy the benefits and the blessings of true sonship.

Chapter Seven

Addendum

As I was completing this book, I received a phone call from Steve Smallman,[1] who had heard that I was writing about Sonship. We discussed some of the issues briefly, and Steve graciously offered to send me some materials that I did not have—which he quickly did. While there was little in them that was new, some things say more clearly what I have been writing all along. So I determined to note, quote and make a few comments on these.

In the *Harvester*, No. 43, Spring, 1999, page 4 we read,

> Not long ago, I had the opportunity to go to an executive retreat of the *Evangelical Foreign Missions Association* of EFMA, of which WHM is a member. One of the speakers was a prominent Christian leader. In one of his talks he told us that he had learned to make repentance a lifestyle, and that rather than being a burden, it was an experience of joy because it meant starting every morning by going back to the cross and being "reconverted." I understood exactly what he meant, because it sounded so much like one of World Harvest's favorite admonitions—"Preach the gospel to yourself every day."

Granted that we are all sinners, granted that repentance should have a significant place in our lives, the question still

---

[1] Smallman is the Director of World Harvest Mission which promotes Sonship™.

arises, isn't this going much too far? To commend the speaker's comment about lifestyle repentance and being "reconverted" every morning, is like saying to a child "I'm going to spank you at the start of every day because I know that you'll need a spanking before the day is over!" There is nothing about living such a lifestyle in the Scriptures. To make repentance a "joy" rather than an experience of sorrow at having offended a heavenly Father also seems strange (cf. II Corinthians 6:8-12; 12:21). And, while we're at it, let's note that a lifestyle of repentance is like constantly living a family life that majors on seeking forgiveness from one's father. If repentance becomes a lifestyle—something the Bible knows nothing about—it is no longer biblical repentance. Biblical repentance is always connected to offenses in attitude and action from which one wishes to turn. It is a change of mind that leads to a change of life. Again, there is nothing here about the works that follow repentance and that are the evidence that it is genuine. It seems that repentance is considered a technique that is followed *in the abstract*. There is nothing concrete mentioned in all of this. Moreover, if this reductionistic view of repentance is accepted, repentance becomes so routine that it no longer possesses the characteristics of true repentance. It has been sanitized into a routine, and that means it no longer resembles biblical repentance at all.

The quotation just cited confirms what I said in an earlier chapter about Sonshippers repenting and preaching the gospel to one's self again and again. The "admonition" to do so has become a slogan that describes an extra-biblical ritual.

Consider a second item sent by director Smallman. On page 23 of an unpublished D. Min. thesis by John Wade we read,

> Christians who pursue holiness (Heb. 12:14) apart from a constant, conscious resting in their free justification are doomed to frustration and failure.

What does this mean? Where is this taught by the apostles? Hebrews says nothing of the sort. What does he mean by "resting" in one's "free justification" in a "constant, conscious" manner? Perhaps Mr. Wade will tell us when he completes his dissertation. But the words are nearly unintelligible. The best that I can make of them is that moment by moment one is to be thinking about his justification in Christ and somehow this will lead him on to satisfaction and success rather than frustration and failure. Once more, it is contemplation of and some sort of dependence (resting?) upon justification, rather than the study and application of the Word of God to daily tasks in the spirit of prayer, that is supposed to bring success to our endeavors for Jesus Christ. In all of this, we may observe again the Bible is omitted.

In Vol. 1, No. 1, Spring 1999 of a WHM Newsletter article entitled "Soul Food" Steve Smallman wrote,

> Furthermore, if we derive strength for ministry through feeding on the gospel, that is exactly how we are to strengthen those to whom we minister (II Timothy 2:2).

Obviously, II Timothy 2:2 says nothing of the sort. Moreover, the context around the verse adds nothing either. However, in a near cavalier manner of using Scripture, Smallman tells us that Paul teaches that his admonition "You, my son, be strong in the grace that is in Christ Jesus" means ministers need "to be drawing strength to serve from the grace that is in Christ," and that "the verse makes it very clear that we find that grace in the gospel." It is only by desperately searching for passages of Scripture to support a preexistent view that one can "find" support in Paul's words. *Very clearly*, the passages referred to do *not* teach that men in the ministry are to draw grace from the gospel. The grace that they need is found in Christ Himself. Nothing in the passages referred to even hints at the Sonship view.

But now notice the expression "feeding on the gospel."
Beyond the fact that it is a curious one not found in the Bible, it
sets forth a concept that no one would ever have dreamed of
finding in II Timothy had he not been looking for it. Once more
we see that Sonship uses the Bible as a "support" for its already
pre-formed doctrines rather than as the Source from which to
form them.

On page 2 of the same Newsletter Barry Henning says that
"the Gospel is the central driving force in the life of the believer
and the [his] church." But we have seen earlier in this book that
the good news of Christ's death and resurrection is a fact to be
believed, not a force upon which to draw. To keep leaning on
one's adoption rather than striving by the Spirit to understand
and conform to the Word of God seems to place a premium on
ignorance and failure rather than on knowledge and competence.
Why isn't it Jesus Christ, addressing us in the Bible about how to
glorify God, that is the driving force of the Christian life? Love
from and for Him is what should "constrain" us.

That Smallman, WHM and Sonship have in mind radically
changing the church is evident from the editor's "Note" in the
Newsletter just cited. On page 3, he writes:

> In our renewal work, World Harvest is deliberately
> trying to push for a "paradigm shift" in what our
> ministries look like. Not surprisingly, this leads to
> controversy as we challenge long-held assumptions,
> and make mistakes ourselves.

When long-held assumptions are challenged the one doing the
challenging had better be very sure that he is right in doing so.
Otherwise he may upset congregations, mission boards and indi-
viduals in very serious ways (that is exactly what I think is happening). What are these "long-held assumptions"? They are the
reformation doctrines adhered to by the Protestant churches. To
challenge such is a serious matter. Yet, it is almost in a casual

manner that Smallman speaks of challenging these doctrines and
causing controversy thereby. Moreover, he seems not to find it a
problem that mistakes are made in the challenge. Let people's
lives be the experimental ground upon which Sonship finds its
way! Something is wrong here too!

In speaking of faith in the gospel Smallman writes about
"having seen this presented over and over."[1] I have heard con-
firming evidence from some who sat under Sonship teaching.
They claim that Sonship has but one string on its guitar. Reading
the literature not only backs this up, but it also shows how shallow the teaching is and that there is little or no true Bible exposition. Yet, the next sentence in the article urges, "But let me
encourage all of you, in that you are teachers, to dig deeper into
this wonderful truth—both to understand it for others and to live
it out yourselves." In other words, play that one string more
loudly! Pluck it for all you are worth! Keep on repeating and
repeating the same thing over and over until you convince yourself that there is more to adoption than what there actually is.
More and more of the same—but thicker and thicker! One hopes
because of this meaningless redundancy Sonship will soon begin
to lose adherents who discover how little there is to it after all!
When you dig in a shallow stream you soon hit bottom.

Harping on the theme, Smallman writes,

> we need to recognize that the essential content of
> our discipleship is to be **the gospel**—taking *people
> who have believed the gospel back into the gospel
> again and again.*[2] [emphases his]

Jesus seemed to think differently about discipling. He spoke of
making disciples (obviously through the preaching of the gos-

---

[1] Newsletter, p.4.
[2] A paper by S. Smallman, GOSPEL DISCIPLING—THE CRYING NEED
OF THE HOUR, November, 1997, p. 1.

pel), but then went on to urge that we teach them "to observe
whatsoever I have commanded you" (Matthew 28:20).

On page 5 of the paper (just cited) we are referred to Romans
1:16. Then we are informed that the verse "should be understood
as empowering believers through every aspect of that salvation."
This radical reinterpretation of the passage might be plausible
but for the phrase that is omitted ("to the Jew first and also to the
Greek."). This phrase plainly identifies Paul's intent as evangelistic—not edificational. It is the evangelistic strategy that he
used throughout the book of Acts. Smallman writes that "at the
core of our ministry is the exposure of the depth of the flesh—so
none of us should be surprised at what any of us are capable
of."[1] But this emphasis, together with the avoidance of the biblical emphasis on obedience (which is so evident in the literature)
can become an excuse for laxity. And in addition to this fact, it is
serious business to delve into the depths of evil. That is what the
Lord Jesus taught the members of the church of Thyatira who
were getting mixed up in what some called "the depths of Satan"
(Revelation 2:24). Along with its emphasis on special guidance
and "openness" in groups, it could be a devastating thing for
some to get caught up in this "core" ministry of the "exposure of
the depth of our flesh." While I shall not investigate it in this
book, I would seriously question Sonship's understanding of the
Pauline concept of the flesh as well.

I could go on—and on, and on. But I won't. There is just
more and more of the same. Instead, I would implore you to ask
yourself, what about the "commands" in the New Testament?
What of discipling people to "observe" them? What of the hundreds and hundreds of specific exhortations the Bible contains?
Are we merely to "rest" in justification, revisit the way of salvation again and again, or is there more to Christianity? Lay aside
the Sonship materials that you may have been perusing and take

---

[1] Letter to the writer, May 5, 1999, p. 1.

time to read the Bible once again. Notice any difference? Clearly, there is a world of difference. Can you see it—or have you been so brainwashed by hearing and repeating the same slogans over and over again that you cannot?

Chapter Eight

Conclusion

Sonship is spreading. In time, if it hasn't happened already, you may soon be confronted with its claims. When you are, remember, the desire for more faithful Christian living that you will encounter in Sonship is a good one. The means for attaining it that Sonship presents are not good. Instead of urging Christians to greater obedience (Sonship demeans this as sinful "trying harder"), Sonshippers will urge you to adopt their ritual of preaching the gospel again to yourself. That, we have seen, is an unbiblical approach to Christian growth. Moreover, when you hear Sonship advocates speak of repentance, ask yourself, "What kind of repentance is it that does not lead to a determined, Spirit-motivated effort to turn about and go the other way?" While the New Testament term *metanoia* means "a change of mind," the Old Testament word *shuv* means "a turning about so as to head in the opposite direction." Together, they constitute the full, biblical concept of repentance. Nothing less can be accepted.

Because (as we have seen) Sonship's emphasis is all one-sided (and, therefore, distorted), we cannot follow its lead. It will take one down the tortured paths that lead to the failure and disappointment that the Millers experienced. Do not abandon the historic, Reformed view of sanctification for this new, inadequate and twisted one. Ultimately, you will regret it, as some already have.

There is no reason to substitute the supposed "insights" of this new view for the tried and true approach of Christians throughout the years. Indeed, what you are trading off is the correct understanding of Christian growth and experience for some-

thing that cannot commend itself biblically or make good on its
claims. I urge you, therefore, give full consideration to that fact
before you plunge ahead into something that you may later—
after great confusion, sorrow and regret—find necessary to
abandon.

If you already have become a devotee of Sonship, I ask you
to examine the facts. You were promised great joy, emotional
satisfaction, and a deeper lifestyle. Have you really found these
things in Sonship? I ask you to judge whether, instead, you have
found yourself more often than not having to engender such joy
and emotion yourself? Have you been overcoming sins? Are you
growing by grace? Do you study the Bible more faithfully than
before? Are you more obedient to Biblical injunctions? Is your
marriage in better shape? Do you truly experience the growth of
the Spirit's fruit?

If you cannot answer these questions in the affirmative, perhaps you should reexamine your commitment to the Sonship
movement. I urge you to do so, rather than to go on pumping up
enthusiasm for something that does not really deliver on its
claims. You may find that you have been sold a bill of goods!

If you have not yet reached the point where you have seen
through the movement for what it is, I urge you not to throw this
book away. The time may come when you will need to reread it.
At any rate, it is out of great concern that I write this to you.
How great the potential for harm that Sonship may do to individ-
uals and to the Church is not yet entirely clear. It is still in its
early days. But the time will come when we shall be able to
examine its fruit more satisfactorily. My prediction is that unless
its impact can be blunted, the damage will be considerable.

I recognize that what I have written is not comprehensive.
But I believe that it gets at the heart of the matters that matter. I
pray that it may help you.

Appendix

Since it is impossible to determine what the "openness" in Sonship™ groups is like in any given instance, it might be well for attendees to consider the following reprint of an article I wrote over 25 years ago.

Group Therapy— or Slander?[1]

Articles recently appearing in national magazines have emphasized the rapid growth of a modern phenomenon known as The Group. These articles have given the general public a candid look at the procedures that are used at the more lavish and well-known centers in which group "encounters" are taking place (cf. the article in *Time Magazine*, November 9, 1970, pp. 54-58). These articles themselves should be the most potent means of discouraging Christians from participation in such activities. The fundamentally non-Christian purposes and character of the activities in question should be apparent to every instructed Christian. Shedding all principles and inhibitions (even those Christian virtues that are appropriate to normal everyday living), sinful men and women are encouraged to express their here-and-now feelings with abandon in whatever manner they may see fit. The then-and-there perspective to which responsibility before God is attached is perilously forgot-

---

[1] Published originally in *The Presbyterian Guardian*, Vol. 40, No. 2, February 1971. This article was revised extensively for inclusion in *The Big Umbrella* (now out of print).

ten. Resentments and bitterness may be vented with vehement hostility; sexually erotic contacts are encouraged in stimulating and provocative contexts. Literally, there are no holds barred. The desperation of unbelieving psychiatrists (if they cannot be charged with more reprehensible motives) at least seems apparent in these attempts to rid their patients of their cultural and religious "hang ups."

It is not, therefore, with the more obviously extreme varieties of Encounter Groups, T Groups, Sensitivity Training Groups, Human Potential Workshops or whatever name a local variation of Carl Rogers' Esalen-based movement may assume, that I am concerned in this article. Rather, I should like to call your attention to the less spectacular and, therefore, potentially more dangerous backwash now beginning to appear in schools, industry, mental institutions, counseling centers, seminaries, and even in Christian churches. These groups have not received the publicity allotted to the national organizations, which they often reflect, but they also are growing with astounding rapidity. Because participants in these less spectacular groups do not ordinarily disrobe or engage in the more esoteric practices of others who are involved in the better known programs, they may suppose that they are participating in an entirely different activity. Preachers themselves, unwittingly, may adopt procedures that are based upon non-Christian presuppositions.[1]

In addition to the "Encounter" groups that are based upon the non-Christian idea that an uncontrolled release of emotion is desirable, there are other forms of group "therapy" that stress confession and openness (honesty). One example of the latter is O. Hobart Mowrer's Integrity Groups (the distinction is becoming blurred even here, however, since just last year [1970] Mow-

---

[1] Cf. the recent Reformed Ecumenical Synod Report on Race (Chicago, March 2-5, 1971): "That a model be prepared for facilitating attitude change ('mind liberation'). . . the teacher would encourage them to express their feelings. . ." p. 6.

rer "discovered" the need for "involvement." That discovery has moved his confession groups closer to the Esalen movement. He now calls for shouting, crying, and "reaching out" to touch other members of the group). It is this latter sort of group, stressing confession in combination with elements of the encounter or sensitivity groups, that seems to be making a significant appeal to Christians. Seminarians and youth groups, for instance, are now being subjected to such group programs. Since it is impossible to describe the endless variations upon the several basic themes that run throughout these groups, it might be most profitable to gather together some important biblical criteria by which any local manifestation of group encounter or therapy may be judged. And since space here is limited, I shall then focus upon only one of these in depth.

Among the many trenchant issues that might be mentioned are the following:

(1) There is no biblical warrant for systematically unlacing another person and throwing his stuffing around the room in order to ventilate one's own hostilities in a selfish attempt to find relief for himself. It is really quite unnecessary to take other people apart or tell them off in the name of honesty and openness. Biblical honesty is of a different sort, and neither requires nor allows such activity. Consider James 5:9, 10; 4:11; Ephesians 4:27-32; Proverbs 10:12; Philippians 2:4; Romans 15:1-3.

(2) "Openness" of the sort frequently encountered in such groups is not a biblical concept. While believers should "speak the truth" to one another "in love," they must not be so open that they may feel free to discuss any and all matters, without distinction or exception, with anyone in any group. Ephesians 5:3, 12 seems pertinent to this problem.

(3) Christians must carefully select the groups with which they associate intimately. They may not so associate with any group indiscriminately. The Christian's relationship to the church as a biblical group bound together by the Spirit in the

bonds of the gospel, the truth and the love of God, differs radically from his relationship to other groups. It is questionable
whether it is even possible for a Christian to consider seriously
participation in an encounter or therapy group composed of non-
Christians on the basis of the membership of the group alone. On
the other hand, there is also the necessity to demonstrate the
need or biblical warrant for Christians to sponsor encounter and
therapy sessions composed of Christians alone.

(4) The Bible does not suggest that people with unaltered
sinful life patterns should be dealt with in such groups (apart
from groups gathered together to listen to the proclamation of
the Word). Indeed, Matthew 18 seems to require that problems
be kept on a personal level if possible. II Thessalonians 3:14, 15
and I Corinthians 5:9-11 seem to be of relevance.

(5) Biblical wisdom indicates that one must not rely upon
sinfully rebellious and biblically confused persons for counsel.
On this matter, read Proverbs 13:20. Should the blind lead the
blind?

(6) Such groups tend to develop divisive loyalties that do not
serve the cause of Christ. The warnings of Titus 3:10 and
Romans 16:17 are of importance in evaluating the tendencies of
very "open" groups which, in order to preserve their openness,
may find it necessary to become very tight-knit. Specialized
groups can too readily be substituted for the proper group, the
Church itself.

These and other similar issues may be raised about some of
the groups to which many earnest Christians have been attracted
in search of help. I cannot discuss them more fully here, but I do
want to devote the remainder of this article to a serious objection
that may be raised with regard to many of the confession type
groups that are now beginning to appear under Christian aus-
pices. That objection is that there is (unintentionally) a grave
amount of gossip or slander sanctioned and carried on under the
aegis of the Church.

Slander and gossip are specifically forbidden in many places in the Bible (e.g., Titus 3:2, Eph. 4:31). Nevertheless, what happens in some groups is, in my opinion, nothing short of a violation of these divine injunctions. Members of the group are frequently encouraged to "tell their story" to persons who, until that moment, have no involvement or interest in their affairs. Yet now, before strangers, they are encouraged (sometimes coerced by group pressure) to reveal the details not only of their own foibles and failures (that sort of thing might be permissible under carefully controlled conditions), but also those of persons who have no means of knowing that their privacy is being invaded, who are powerless to stop it, and who are not present to correct the one-sided account that inevitably is given. Even in those groups in which one is supposed to concentrate upon his *own* sins (and this is by no means the prevailing approach), it is usually necessary to talk about others behind their backs in order to tell one's own story. It is hard for persons in such a group to avoid gossiping. Since our major problems in life mostly have to do with our relationships to others, it is nearly impossible to be "open" about ourselves and not involve others.

Can we dump our personal resentments and complaints on the table before strangers without slandering others? Specifically, should young people at a Christian college or seminary be encouraged to spill the beans about their parents, their brothers and sisters, their pastors, and other young persons back home? Should wives be provided opportunity to discuss the failures of their husbands behind their backs? Should men in a confession-oriented group disclose intimate details about their marriages and then declare to their wives that loyalty to the group supersedes the loyalties of the marriage relationship and, therefore, prohibits them from disclosing what they said?

A group context of this sort often encourages group members to make accusations and charges apart from the benefit of the safeguards of both the informal and official biblical procedures involved in reconciliation and discipline. When the group meets without these safeguards, it may operate as a kangaroo court. Without demanding adequate evidence or witnesses, without providing for a defense by the party whose name and character may be at stake, the group allows a member to make charges that it frequently accepts at face value. Judgment is given and action is often recommended on the basis of this one-sided information. In effect, in his absence and usually in complete ignorance of the fact, a brother in Christ who may be quite innocent of the charges is tried, convicted and judged *in absentia*. Great damage may be done as a result, since the group has failed to heed the warning of Proverbs 18:17, "He who states his cause first seems right until another comes to examine him" (Berkeley).

Talking to others who have not previously been involved in a problem about those who are is nothing less than the substitution of a human methodology for the divinely-ordained procedures outlined in Matthew 5:23, 24; 18:15-17. There God says that a Christian believer who is offended by another must go to him and attempt to bring about a biblical resolution of the matter leading to a reconciliation of the parties. (If he has wronged his brother, then he still is obligated to go and seek reconciliation.) Jesus specifically requires that the matter be kept in the strictest privacy: "If your brothers sins, go and reprove him in private" (Matt. 18:15, NASV). Only reluctantly, when reconciliation cannot be achieved by private consultation, is one allowed to involve others—and then only one or two. These men are not pictured as members of a therapy or encounter group, but rather as counselors who should be "heard." If at length their efforts also fail, they become witnesses and official discipline is required. Only then does the matter become public, i.e., known to the Church (this probably means known to the eldership, who represent the church; not in the first instance to the entire congregation).

I do not want to convey the idea that I am opposed to groups as such. To oppose groups is like opposing motherhood or sunsets. God structured a group-type society from the creation. What I want to oppose is the abuse of groups. All sorts of group work may be biblical and, therefore, profitable. One of our tasks as Christians is to develop every form of group that is compatible with and, therefore, useful to the Kingdom of God. But it is also our task to detect and warn against every abuse of the group that appears.

There is a biblically legitimate form of confession group: such a group should be as large as but no larger than the group of persons who actually are parties to the offense. These may be as few as two, as in the examples given in Matthew 5 and 18. That is to say, a biblical grouping provides for the possibility of reconciliation and seeks it as its end. The group must, therefore, be composed of the estranged parties. Confession is wrongly conceived of when it is considered to be an end in itself. Unbiblical groups distort confession, making it a personal catharsis that occurs through ventilation. Confession rather must be seen as a means leading toward forgiveness and reconciliation. It is a loving act in which the other person is prominently in view, not merely one's self (Eph. 4:32).

Groups stressing confession in a non-reconciliation context often impede reconciliation. Ventilation temporarily reduces the pressure of the guilt of unconfessed sin and estrangement. The relief is temporary, to be sure, because in the long run ventilation increases one's sense of guilt. This is true since the original problem has not been solved by ventilation, the poor relationship has not been bettered, and now ventilation itself has added the guilt of gossip or slander to an already overburdened conscience.

The amazing growth of groups must be explained as a multi-factored phenomenon. For instance, new elements that characterize our modern mobile society, such as the virtual dissolution of village community life, have contributed to an acute sense of need for fellowship and friendship. After all, God made man a social creature who should find his fellowship in groups, like the family and the Church, that were ordained by God for such a purpose. There is nothing wrong with the people of God grouping together for worship, for mutual instruction and encouragement, for service and for fellowship. God Himself has endorsed and encouraged such grouping (Heb. 10:24, 25). It is not the idea of a group that must be opposed, but the distortion of the biblical idea. The problem with such therapy and encounter groups as I have described is that since they are unbiblical, they meet for the wrong purposes, they exist on the wrong basis, they operate with the wrong personnel and they use the wrong methods.

There is one note yet to sound: the Church has failed in large measure to help Christians meet their social needs and interpersonal relations in a truly biblical manner. It is time for the Church to begin to do so. The best protection against the baneful effects of unbiblical group activities is the blessing that flows from biblically oriented groups. This blessing will come only by making provision for all of those crucial social needs that God implanted in man. Many of these elements have been neglected. The Church must provide for its members more wholesome social contact, must preach, teach and encourage specifically the mutual ministry of all believers to one another in which the Spirit's gifts are used for the benefit of all, and finally must reinstitute both informal and formal discipline among its members for the glory of God, the welfare of the Church, and the reclamation and reconciliation of offenders. Encounter and therapy groups are not the answer.